![DK] **Watch me grow**

Kitten

LONDON, NEW YORK, MUNICH,
MELBOURNE and DELHI

Written and edited by Lisa Magloff
Designed by Sonia Moore and Mary Sandberg
Publishing Manager Sue Leonard
Managing Art Editor Clare Shedden
Jacket Design Tony Chung
Picture Researcher Liz Moore
Production Shivani Pandey
DTP Designer Almudena Díaz

First American Edition, 2005

Published in the United States by
DK Publishing, Inc.
375 Hudson Street
New York, New York 10014

05 06 07 08 09 10 9 8 7 6 5 4 3 2 1

A Cataloging-in-Publication record for this book
is available from the Library of Congress.

ISBN 0-7566-1156-3

Color reproduction by Media, Development and Printing, Ltd.
Printed and bound in China by South China Printing Co, Ltd.

Discover more at

www.dk.com

Contents

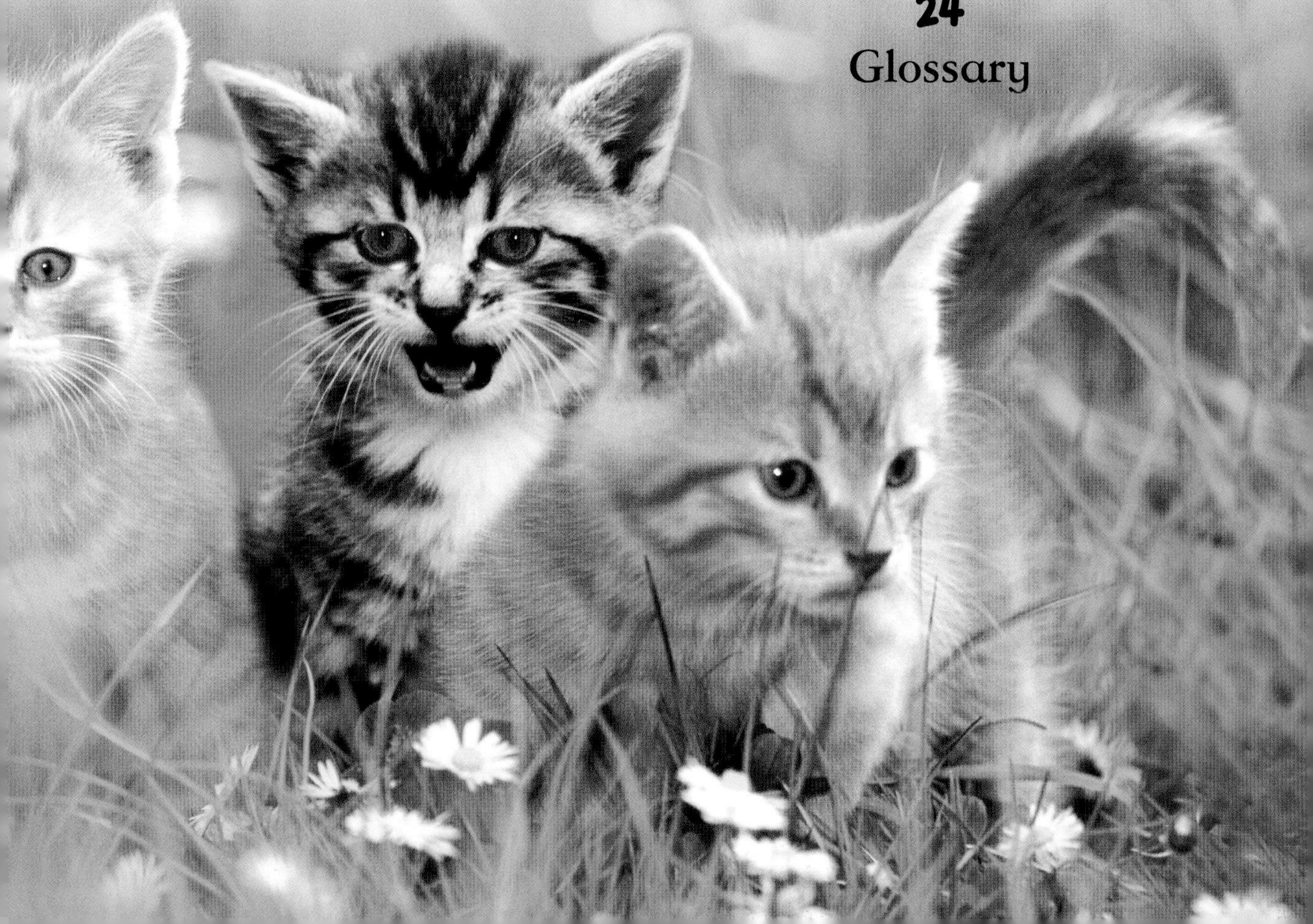

I'm a cat

I can live almost anywhere. I have soft fur to keep me warm and protect me. I love to scamper, play, and hunt for mice.

A long, flexible tail helps a cat to balance.

Sharp claws help cats to hunt and to grab things.

Here are Mom and Dad with all our friends and family.

Cats' eyes
can see well
in the dark.

Lullaby cat
Cats spend most of the
day sleeping. They can
sleep just about any time,
and in any position.

Whiskers also
help cats to
balance.

Now turn the page and watch us grow.....

My Mom and Dad

My Mom and Dad live next door to each other. They met in the garden. Dad had to chase away a lot of other males before he had kittens with Mom.

Keeping clean
Cats love to keep their fur clean and neat. Dad washes himself by licking his paws and then rubbing his face.

This mother cat's tummy is very big because it is almost time for her litter of kittens to be born.

I'm one day old

I'm hungry. It's time for me to nurse. Mom helps us all to find her milk by gently pushing us with her paws. It's a tight squeeze, but we all fit in.

The mother cat lies quietly while her litter drinks.

Newborns
For the first few days, the kittens spend almost all of their time lying together in a pile, keeping warm.

Kitten facts

· ·

🐈 The kittens can't see, but they can smell where Mom is.

🐈 Newborn kittens sleep most of the time.

🐈 During feeding, the kittens will purr if they are getting enough milk.

Mom washes us

We are too little to wash ourselves,
so Mom does it by licking us all over.
This not only keeps our fur clean,
it also makes us feel safe and happy.

A free ride
Baby kittens can't walk,
so when Mom wants to
move them, she picks them
up gently in her mouth.
They hold still and tuck
up their legs.

It's my sister's turn to be cleaned.

I'm two weeks old

At last! My eyes are open, so I can finally see where I am going. Now I can start to practice wobbly walking. I can also hear much better than I could when I was born.

Great! Now I can see my brothers and sisters!

Night sight

When they are grown up, these kittens will see better at night than we can. They will use this super vision to hunt at night.

The kittens call to Mom so she always knows where they are.

This little kitten is learning to stand up.

Now I can play

I'm four weeks old and full of energy.
My brothers and sisters and I love to play.
We learn to pounce by practicing on Mom's
tail, but I don't think she likes it very much.

Ready, set, go!
Kittens will play
with almost
anything that
moves. This is
how they learn
to hunt.

Mom's tail makes a
handy toy for the kittens.

Lunch bunch
The kittens are still nursing, but they are also starting to eat solid food.

I think it's time for you to play outside...

Play-fighting

My brother and I pretend to fight
with each other. It's just a game,
and no one gets hurt.

I hide in the grass and wait to pounce.

Here I come!

The kitten's tail helps her to balance while she leaps.

This is just play, so the kittens don't use their claws.

Scaredy cat

This kitten has never seen a frog before. He is scared, so he is puffing himself up and trying to look bigger.

Let's explore

We are ten weeks old and are very curious. This branch is a fun place to explore. Climbing up was easy, but it will be harder to climb down.

Is this the way down?

Look at me now. I'm 12 weeks old and very grown up.

Head over heels

Cats almost always land on their feet. This is because they can turn around in the air.

The circle of life goes
around and around

Now you know how I turned
into a grown-up cat.

My friends from around the world

Siamese cats love to talk and will meow all day long.

The Red Persian cat has long, silky hair in a solid rusty color.

Can you see why I am called

The Mackerel Tabby Oriental loves to cuddle and sit on laps.

My cat friends from around the world come in lots of different colors and sizes.

Sphynx cats have short, fine "peach-fuzz" instead of hair.

Manx cats come in many colors, but do not have a tail.

I'm a Dilute

Calico cat

a Blue Shorthair cat?

Kitten facts
....

🐈 Cats smell with a special organ on the roof of their mouth.

🐈 Cats step with both left legs, then both right legs when they walk or run.

🐈 Cats spend one-third of their time grooming their fur.

Glossary

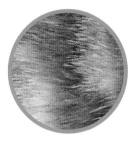

Fur
The thick coat of hair that covers and protects a cat.

Pounce
To leap or jump on an object or another animal, like a mouse.

Litter
A group of kittens that are all born at the same time.

Purr
The noise a cat makes when it is happy and full of food.

Nurse
When kittens drink milk from their mother's breast.

Tongue
Cats' tongues are very rough, so they can use them to lick.

Acknowledgments
The publisher would like to thank the following for their kind permission to reproduce their photographs:
(Key: a=above; c=center; b=below; l=left; r=right; t=top)
1 Powerstock: Frank Lukasseck c. 2-3 Zefa Visual Media: Frank Lukasseck. 3 Powerstock: Martin Rugner c. 4 Getty Images: Taxi cfl. 4-5 Steven Moore Photography. 4-5 Warren Photographic: Jane Burton x2. 5 Corbis: Helen King cl. 5 Getty Images: Stone tc; Taxi cra. 6 DK Images: Dave King cbl. 6 Steven Moore Photography: cl. 6-7 Steven Moore Photography. 7 DK Images: Jane Burton l, r. 8 DK Images: Jane Burton, bcl. 8-9 DK Images: Jane Burton. 8-9 Steven Moore Photography. 10 OSF/photolibrary.com: IPS Photo Index cb. 10 Warren Photographic: Jane Burton bcr. 11 Warren Photographic: Jane Burton c. 12 Warren Photographic: Jane Burton, cbl. 12-13 Steven Moore Photography. 12-13 Warren Photographic: Jane Burton. 13 Nature Picture Library Ltd: Pete Oxford tl. 14 Warren Photographic: Jane Burton cbr. 14-15 Steven Moore Photography. 14-15 Warren Photographic: Jane Burton.

15 Steven Moore Photography: tl. 15 Warren Photographic: Jane Burton tl. 16 Powerstock: age fotostock cla. 16-17 Powerstock: Martin Rugner/age fotostock. 17 DK Images: Geoff Brightling bc. 17 Steven Moore Photography: bcr. 17 Warren Photographic: Jane Burton br. 18-19 Warren Photographic: Jane Burton. 19 N.H.P.A.: Agence Nature r. 19 Warren Photographic: Jane Burton bl. 20 Alamy Images: Isobel Flynn c. 20 Warren Photographic: Jane Burton cla, ca, cra, crb, bc, bcl, bcr, car, cfl, cfr. 21 OSF/photolibrary.com: Dave Kingdon/IndexStock t. 21 Warren Photographic: Jane Burton cb. 22 Warren Photographic: Jane Burton cb. 22 DK Images: Dave King cla, cra; 22 Warren Photographic: Jane Burton tl. 22-23 DK Images: Marc Henrie. 23 DK Images: Dave King tr; Marc Henrie ca. 23 Powerstock: Martin Rugner/age fotostock br. 24 DK Images: Jane Burton cla, clb. 24 OSF/photolibrary.com: cbr. 24 Powerstock: Martin Rugner/age fotostock car. 24 Warren Photographic: Jane Burton cla, car.
All other images © Dorling Kindersley
For further information, see www.dkimages.com